ANIMAL HOMES

McGraw-Hill
Children's Publishing
A Division of The **McGraw·Hill** Companies

This edition published in the United States in 2002 by
Peter Bedrick Books, an imprint of
McGraw-Hill Children's Publishing,
A Division of The McGraw-Hill Companies
8787 Orion Place
Columbus, OH 43240

www.MHkids.com

ISBN 0-87226-688-5

Library of Congress Cataloging-in-Publication Data is on file with the publisher.

Animal Homes created and produced by

McRae Books

via de' Rustici, 5, Florence (Italy)
tel. +39 055 264 384
fax +39 055 212 573
e-mail: mcrae@tin.it

Project Manager: Anne McRae
Graphic Design: Marco Nardi
Illustrations: Fiammetta Dogi, Antonella Pastorelli, Ivan Stalio, Thomas Troyer
Picture Research: Holly Willis
Editing: Joanna Buck
Layout and cutouts: Adriano Nardi, Laura Ottina

Color separations: Litocolor (Florence)
Printed and bound in Italy

2 3 4 5 6 7 8 9 10 MCR 06 45 04 03 02

AFRICAN GRASSLANDS

Text by Christina Longman
Illustrations by Fiammetta Dogi

PETER BEDRICK BOOKS

Table of Contents

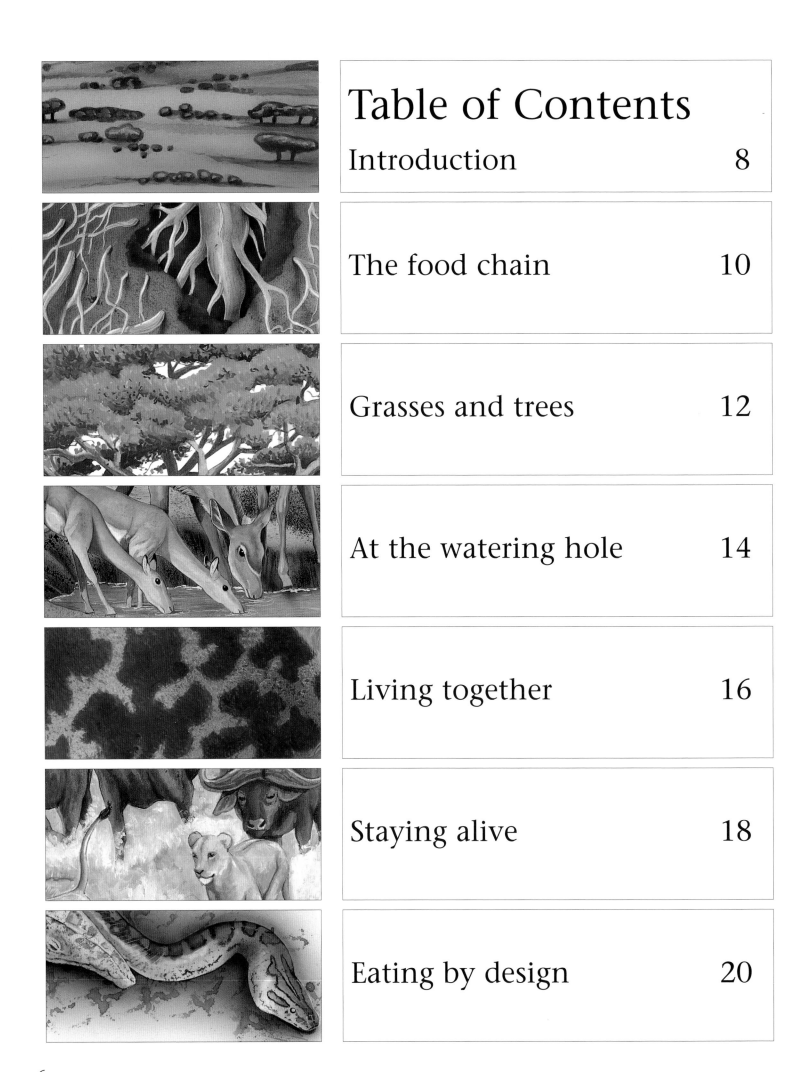

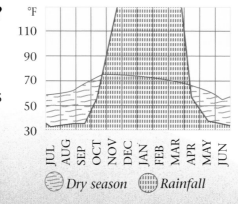

AFRICA
Sahara Desert

Masai Mara

Equator

Serengeti

ATLANTIC OCEAN

Namib Desert

The green areas on the above map show the locations of the grasslands in Africa. Most of Africa's large wildlife species live in these regions.

Introduction

About 25 million years ago, almost all of Africa was covered with thick woodlands. But as the climate changed and less rain began to fall, the thick forests gave way to grasslands, which were better suited to the drier climate. African grasslands, called **savannas**, are one of the world's most exciting **ecosystems**. They are home to a wonderful range of animals that move constantly as they follow the rains in search of new grass and other food.

Where are tropical grasslands?

Tropical grasslands are found on both sides of the equator between the rain forests and deserts. They cover about 6 million square miles (10 million square kilometers), an area much larger than the size of Australia. Today, the most famous grasslands are in eastern Africa, in National Game Parks like Serengeti and Masai Mara. They can also be found in Australia, India, and South America.

°F
110
90
70
50
30

JUL AUG SEP OCT NOV DEC JAN FEB MAR APR MAY JUN

Dry season   Rainfall

Climate

The savanna has a warm climate all year round. The red line on the graph at left shows average monthly temperatures on the savanna in Zimbabwe that range from 60°F (15°C) in June to 72°F (22°C) in October and November. The green area on the graph shows the most rain fall in the hotter months when the tropical grasses grow as much as an inch a day!

Carnivores

The savanna is full of meat-eating animals, known as carnivores. Crocodiles are carnivorous reptiles. In the savannas, they hide at water holes and rivers, waiting to attack their victims with their powerful jaws and tails. Crocodiles have sharp teeth, but they cannot chew and must swallow their dinner whole!

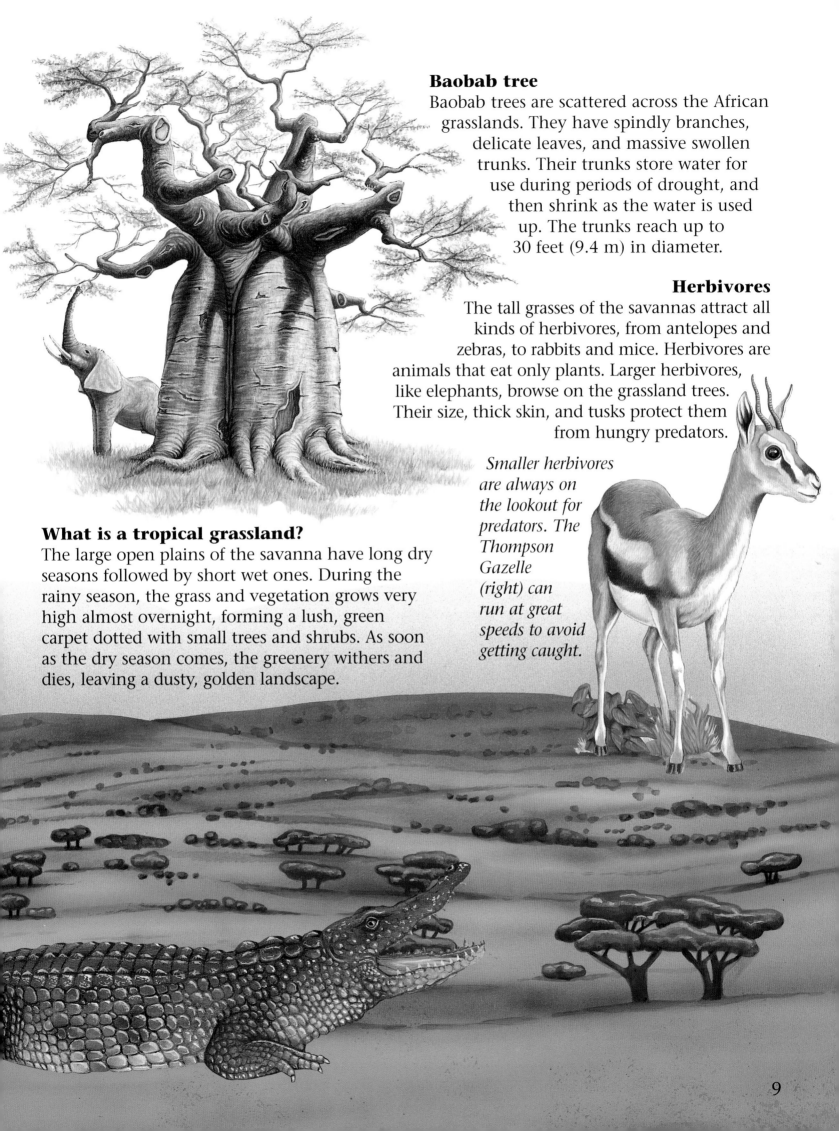

Baobab tree

Baobab trees are scattered across the African grasslands. They have spindly branches, delicate leaves, and massive swollen trunks. Their trunks store water for use during periods of drought, and then shrink as the water is used up. The trunks reach up to 30 feet (9.4 m) in diameter.

Herbivores

The tall grasses of the savannas attract all kinds of herbivores, from antelopes and zebras, to rabbits and mice. Herbivores are animals that eat only plants. Larger herbivores, like elephants, browse on the grassland trees. Their size, thick skin, and tusks protect them from hungry predators.

Smaller herbivores are always on the lookout for predators. The Thompson Gazelle (right) can run at great speeds to avoid getting caught.

What is a tropical grassland?

The large open plains of the savanna have long dry seasons followed by short wet ones. During the rainy season, the grass and vegetation grows very high almost overnight, forming a lush, green carpet dotted with small trees and shrubs. As soon as the dry season comes, the greenery withers and dies, leaving a dusty, golden landscape.

9

The food chain

All the plants and animals in the savanna ecosystem are linked to each other in some way. The grasslands are an excellent source of food for herbivores. Herbivores, in turn, provide food for carnivores. Scavengers, like jackals and vultures, arrive after the carnivores finish feeding to feast on the leftovers. The droppings from all these savanna animals enrich the soil, helping the grasses to grow again after the dry season. Insects, fungi, and bacteria break down the remains of plants and animals so that the good elements are absorbed back into the soil.

African savanna soil

The savanna soil is usually a rich, red color because of the iron it contains. The hot sun and the wet and dry seasons cause a hard brick-like layer to form on the top layer of soil. This is called a hardpan. Grasses grow above this layer, but many trees cannot break through it to put down roots.

The heavy rains wash away most of the minerals in the soil.

Termite farmers

Termites play an important role in soil formation. These strong insects help to break down the remains of trees. They chew the wood and then use it to grow a fungus inside their mounds. The wood is broken down with the help of a bacteria that they pass on to each other by mouth in their food.

Bacteria and fungi

Bacteria and fungi feed on dead plants and animal remains. The food is broken down so finely that nutrients are returned to the soil. New grass and saplings find the food they need in this rich, organic soil because of these tiny organisms.

10

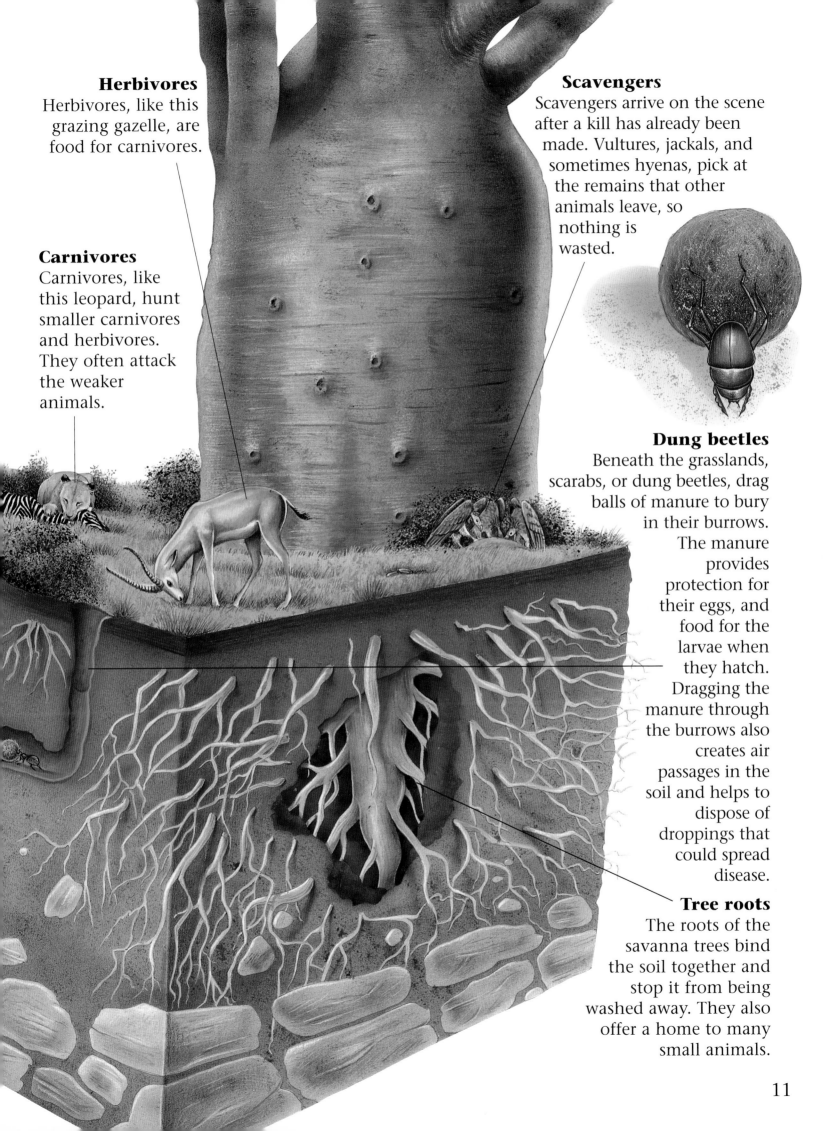

Herbivores
Herbivores, like this grazing gazelle, are food for carnivores.

Carnivores
Carnivores, like this leopard, hunt smaller carnivores and herbivores. They often attack the weaker animals.

Scavengers
Scavengers arrive on the scene after a kill has already been made. Vultures, jackals, and sometimes hyenas, pick at the remains that other animals leave, so nothing is wasted.

Dung beetles
Beneath the grasslands, scarabs, or dung beetles, drag balls of manure to bury in their burrows. The manure provides protection for their eggs, and food for the larvae when they hatch. Dragging the manure through the burrows also creates air passages in the soil and helps to dispose of droppings that could spread disease.

Tree roots
The roots of the savanna trees bind the soil together and stop it from being washed away. They also offer a home to many small animals.

11

Umbrella thorn tree

Shade and safety

The thorny twigs of acacia trees may stop some animals from eating them, but at the same time they offer shade and protection to birds nesting in their branches.

Grasses and trees

The savanna is covered with many different species of grasses and clumps of low trees and shrubs. The plants have adapted to growing in a hot climate and can survive long periods of drought. Taller grasses grow nearer the equatorial forests where rainfall is more abundant, while the shorter grasses grow nearer the deserts. The grasslands not only provide excellent food for herbivores, but also shelter for small animals, like rabbits and mice, and building material for nests.

Zebra

Impala

Gazelle

What are grasses?

Grasses are flowering plants. Most of them die after they have flowered, but their roots survive to grow new plants. If you look closely at a grass plant, you will see its long, thin stem is divided into sections, called nodes. These produce the leaves of the plant. Many tropical grasses can grow very tall. They contain silica, which makes them strong so they can resist the harsh winds blowing across the savanna.

A typical savanna grass

Flowers are pollinated by the wind

Leaf

Rhizome

New plant

Different species of herbivores can all live together in the same area. This is because they all graze or browse on the grasses and trees at different heights and at different times of the day and year.

Survival against the odds

Unlike other plants, grasses grow from the bottom of the stem instead of the top. This means they can quickly grow again after animals have grazed on them or they have been destroyed by fire, high winds, or drought. Many grasses produce rhizomes. These are roots that grow out horizontally just above or below the ground, helping the grasses to spread rapidly.

Acacia trees

Acacia trees are typical of the eastern African savannas. This thorny tree has a flat crown, due to stunted growth during the dry season, and nibbling by animals. The wind blowing through the swollen thorns of the whistling acacia makes a strange, eerie sound that has given the tree its name. Another African species of acacia gives us gum arabic, used in glue and medicines.

Acacia tree

Safe in the trees

Leopards are good climbers and spend much of their time in trees. Up high, they are safe from other predators and can scan the land for prey. They carry their prey, like this unfortunate impala, onto a branch, out of the reach of competitors like lions and jackals.

Planting seeds

Elephant grass and acacia trees have developed special ways to beat the hard soil of the savannas. Their seeds are wrapped in hard, spiral capsules. When the ground warms up, the capsules swell with the heat. They then shrink as the temperature falls at night. This pushes the seeds down into the soil so they are ready to grow as soon as the rains arrive.

Spiral seed cases

Trees in flower

The yellow fever tree was once thought to be the cause of malaria. Its bright flowers grow in the shape of pom-poms, and contrast with its yellow bark.

13

What is a watering hole?

A watering hole may be a lake, a river, a natural spring, or a hole made by an animal. During the dry season, some animals travel miles to find water then return to that same place year after year. Eventually, the watering hole dries up leaving parched, cracked ground. Some lakes disappear completely, exposing vast salt deposits. When the rains fall, the holes fill up again and the animals can return to drink and bathe.

Elephant fun

When water is scarce, elephants often dig their own watering holes. They drink by sucking up water with their flexible trunks and then squirting it into their mouths. Like hippopotamuses and rhinoceroses, elephants wallow in the mud. The dried mud protects their skins from the burning rays of the sun and helps keeps insects away.

Drinking in shifts

Antelopes and zebras are among the first to arrive at the watering holes because they need to drink often. Giraffes and gerenuke get some of the water they need from juicy leaves, so they can go without for longer periods. Many animals take turns at the watering hole, keeping a constant lookout for predators.

Temporary ceasefire

Predators, such as big cats, must drink too. Smaller herbivores can usually tell when these hunters have eaten and will drink at the watering hole as long as they are not too close.

At the watering hole

Stylish drinkers
Because the giraffe's legs are so long, it has to spread its front legs apart, like the giraffe to the left, in order to drink from the watering hole.

All animals need water. As the dry season begins and the land becomes drier, watering holes are the only places where animals can drink. These precious pools of water are filled with wildlife. The dung from the animals attracts insects, which in turn attract birds. As the water evaporates in the hot, sweltering sun, fish, frogs, and snails have less space to hide. They are easy prey for wading birds that move through the water on their long legs, ready to strike their victims with their huge bills.

Sunbathing
Crocodiles bask in the sun at the watering holes, waiting for their next meal to appear.

Back scratching

Olive baboons of eastern Africa live, eat, and sleep together in large numbers. They spend a lot of time grooming each other, which helps to bond the group. Members of the group only groom baboons of a higher social status, so the leader can be groomed by more than one baboon but will never groom another. This sort of organization is called a hierarchy.

Living together

Many animals help each other survive in the harsh conditions of the African savanna. It is easier and safer for them to find food, protect themselves from predators, and take over new territories when they work as part of a team. Animals and plants of different species will work together, as long as there is some benefit for both sides.

Bird cleaners

These little birds, called oxpeckers, perch on herbivores, like this giraffe, eating the fleas and ticks from their hides. The birds get an easy meal, and the giraffe gets rid of its unpleasant guests.

Keeping watch

When a mongoose family hunts, it leaves baby-sitters to guard the den. An adult always sits on top of the mound keeping a lookout for danger. When on the move, the young travel in the middle of the group where they are safe from predators.

Elephant midwives

Elephants live in groups of females and are led by an older female, or matriarch. She leads the herd to food and safety. The elephants work together to raise their young, look after the sick, and even help each other to give birth.

A feast for two

When the African bird called the honey guide (left) finds a bees' nest, it calls a honey badger to open the nest with its strong claws. The bird eats the wax and larvae, while the honey badger, or ratel, feasts on the honey.

Smart trees

Acacia trees risk being eaten by too many herbivores. As a remedy, some of the tree's hollow thorns swell up, offering perfect homes for ants. In return for their homes and fresh food from the tips of the leaves, the ants keep the acacia tree free from other insects and bite any small animals trying to eat the leaves.

Swollen acacia thorn

Colony living

Insects like bees, ants, and termites live in highly organized societies. The queen lays all the eggs and the workers clean, find food, and protect the colony from enemies and natural dangers. In Africa, naked mole-rats (blind, hairless moles) have a similar type of system. They live in underground burrows and serve a queen, who is the only member of the group to give birth.

Risky rides

Turtles sometimes save energy by hitching rides on the backs of crocodiles. They sunbathe and pick up scraps of food that the crocodiles drop. Most of the time, the turtles come and go unnoticed. However, occasionally the crocodiles get an easy meal and the turtles lose out!

17

Staying alive

Staying alive is a full-time job for most herbivores. For protection, most of them live in herds. There are also many ways in which their bodies have adapted to help them survive. Some have long, slender legs to help them outrun predators. Others have coats that blend into the color of their surroundings, making it difficult for predators to see them. Most have exceptional senses of hearing and sight that alert them to a nearby enemy. Despite these advantages, surviving from one day to the next can still be tough.

Ostriches in disguise
Ostriches cannot fly, but they can run very fast on their powerful legs and two-toed feet. When they hold their heads down, their round bodies and long feathers make them look like bushes on the plain, so they escape the predator's scanning eyes.

Blending in
Stripes help to camouflage the zebra in the shrubs and grasses of the savanna landscape. Their stripes also cause confusion when standing in herds, making it difficult for predators to make out a single animal.

Living alarm systems
Cattle egrets, like the ones below, follow herds of wildebeest and other herbivores because they can always get a tasty meal of fleas, ticks, and flies. They act as a warning signal to the animals by becoming agitated as soon as they spot a predator.

Brave buffalo

Buffalo are so strong and have such sharp horns that they will often turn and attack their predators, especially if they are protecting their young. Buffalo are known as one of the most dangerous of the savanna animals.

What long ears you have!

Impalas and other antelopes can swivel their hairy ears to quickly locate where a noise is coming from. This helps them to detect predators creeping up on them. Flapping their large ears also helps them to keep cool and discourage insects from making their homes on their hides.

Animal gymnastics

Springboks can often be seen "stotting," or springing, high into the air. They do this in front of predators to show how fast they can move. The hunter will choose one of the slower individuals that is easier prey. Members of the herd may also recognize the springboks' bobbing white tails as a signal of danger.

Chemical warfare

Soldiers of tree-dwelling nasute termites have developed long, hollow snouts. They squirt an acid spray through their nostrils. The spray becomes sticky and traps invading insects, like ants.

19

Eating by design

There is food for all in the savanna, but the competition is fierce. Fortunately, the amazing variety of animal species means that few have exactly the same diets. Some eat grass, others shrubs and trees, some meat or insects, and some just pick at the leftovers. However, food is not always easy to reach or catch, and many animals have developed special skills for making their mealtimes easier.

Flamingo filters
Flamingos live near water in the savanna. They feed by cleverly filtering food, like crustaceans and plankton, through their beaks. Pigments in the crustaceans give the flamingos their fabulous pink color.

Well-designed scavengers
Marabu storks, like vultures, feed on the corpses of animals. Their heads are bald so that when they eat intestines and inner parts of their meal, their feathers don't get soiled with blood!

Down on their knees
Down on bent knees, the warthog finds a comfortable position for eating and drinking.

Bloodsuckers
Tsetse flies are the pests of the African grasslands. They spread sleeping sickness, a disease that results in prolonged sleep, by biting both people and animals. They feed on blood and can take in huge amounts at any one time, due to their amazing expanding abdomens.

Courageous birds

The long legs of the secretary bird carry it swiftly through the grass in search of snakes, lizards, and small animals. It is easier to spot prey at close range than from the air. Their sharp claws are perfectly adapted to catching snakes, even poisonous ones. They kill their victims with a sharp blow from their beaks.

Good diggers

The bizarre-looking aardvark eats ants and termites. It has large, strong claws for ripping open the hard walls of termite mounds. Its long, sticky tongue is ideal for poking inside the nests to catch the insects.

Far reaching

Up and up stretches the giraffe's long neck, helping it to reach the juiciest leaves at the tops of acacia trees. Giraffes curl their long tongues around the branches and pull the leaves toward their mouths. They don't feel the prickly acacia thorns or ant bites as they feed because of their tough hides.

On the move

Wildebeest live in large herds and travel long distances following the rains in search of good pasture and water. They follow the same routes year after year.

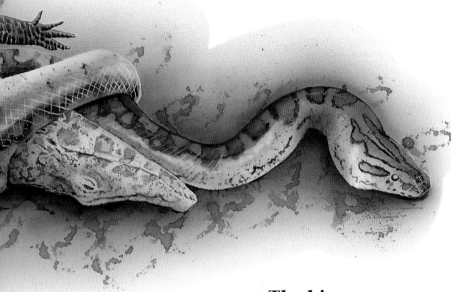

The big squeeze

The African python is a silent killer. It doesn't bite, nor is it poisonous. Instead, the python creeps up, coils itself around its victim's body, and squeezes hard until the victim suffocates. These deadly snakes even attack crocodiles.

Invisible danger

Chameleons can change the color of their skin to blend in with their surroundings. Staying perfectly still, they can swivel their eyes independently of each other to spot an insect. Then they strike out with their long, sticky tongues to catch their prey.

Fierce predators

The deadly predators' list of weapons is endless. Some rely on stealth, strength, and incredible speed. Others track their prey using their exceptional senses of sight, hearing, and smell. Their sharp claws and teeth, or venomous poisons offer little hope of survival for their victims.

Jaws

Resembling harmless logs, crocodiles lie perfectly still in the banks of water. Any passing small- to medium-sized mammal is quickly snapped up in their razor-sharp teeth. They also eat fish and crabs.

Hunting strategies

When times are hard and prey is difficult to catch, lionesses will hunt in groups of two or more. One may crouch in the grass while the other chases the victim towards her hidden partner. Male lions rarely hunt, but they always take the lion's share!

The fastest of all

The elegant cheetah is the fastest of all land animals. It can reach up to 60 miles (about 95 km) an hour, but cannot keep up this pace for long. Over long distances some of its would-be victims do manage to escape.

Swoop from above
Birds of prey have excellent vision and can spot their victims from afar. Buzzards perch on treetops where they scan the ground for small mammals, frogs, and snakes, then swoop on them suddenly. Birds of prey are very useful for keeping down the population of mice and rats.

Teamwork
Although well known for being scavengers, hyenas are efficient hunters, too. They are so strong that a single hyena can pull down a wildebeest by itself. By day they hunt alone or in small groups of two or three, but by night they hunt in large groups.

Straight for the jugular
Leopards are solitary hunters and usually attack at night. They are strong enough to kill antelopes with a swift bite to the neck. However, they often choose smaller prey that other large predators are not interested in.

Spitting
The African spitting cobra fires venom mixed with saliva from a groove in its fangs. It aims at its victim's eyes and temporarily blinds it with its venom.

The night shift

Far from being asleep at night, the savanna comes alive with animals that normally rest by day. "Time-sharing" allows animals that are active by night (nocturnal) and those that are active by day (diurnal) to share the same space and enjoy the same food, but at different times. Nocturnal animals have evolved highly sensitive eyes to see in the dark.

Animal radar

Most bats roost by day and come out at night. They use echolocation to fly around and to find food. Bats send out high-pitched noises through their noses, and the sounds bounce back like echoes. In this way, the bat can then figure out the distance, and even the size of the object in front of it.

The cat's whiskers

Leopards usually hunt at night. They adjust to the dark by dilating their pupils. They have very long, sensitive whiskers to help them feel their way around.

Night-biter

Mosquitoes start biting animals and people at night. Only the females suck blood, and their needle-like mouths are perfectly designed for the job. After she inserts her syringe, she squirts in a special chemical to stop the blood from clotting and sucks it up with her proboscis, or straw.

Safe to come out of the water

Hippopotamuses spend all day in the water to protect their skin from the sun. But, as soon as the sun begins to set, the temperature falls and it's time to come out and graze on the grass. A hippopotamus can travel nearly 20 miles (30 km) in one night.

Open wide
As darkness descends, the nightjars take the place of daytime swallows. They scoop up moths and insects in their short, broad beaks, which can open extremely wide due to a special joint in their jaws.

What big eyes you have!
Bush babies sleep in the trees by day as monkeys scamper about. When the monkeys rest at night, out come the bush babies. Then it's their turn to feed on plants, spiders, insects, and tiny birds. The bush babies' big, round eyes help them to find food in the dark.

Big appetites
Elephants need to eat such a large amount of food that they munch away at night as well as in the day. They are as at home in the darkness as they are in the daylight.

One night flight
On one special night at the beginning of the rainy season, winged termites, the future kings and queens, fly away from their nests to start colonies of their own. Once they land on the ground, they shed their wings and look for a mate, as well as a suitable spot for their new home.

Nests, rests, and burrows

The animals of the African savanna all need to rest sometime. Some simply stretch themselves out on the ground or in the treetops. Others find a special refuge or dig a burrow underground where they can sleep and safely raise their young. Birds and insects are expert builders, weaving, stitching, and gluing to make beautiful homes for themselves.

Lazy zebra
This zebra is taking a nap during the day, but the rest of the herd is awake and on the alert. Later on, the napping zebra will keep watch while another zebra rests.

Sleeping underground
Many small mammals, like gerbils, dig burrows for themselves underground, where they sleep, store food, and raise their young. Sometimes the burrows have more than one entrance, so that the owners can escape when a predator, such as a snake, appears on the scene!

Fried eggs
Ostriches, being large and unable to fly, make their nests on the ground. Although a nest belongs to just one pair (a male and female), other females lay their eggs there, too. The real nest owner pushes the foreign eggs into a ring around the outside of the nest, where they get very hot in the sun and are the first to be taken by a predator.

Living umbrellas
The crowned crane builds a flat nest of sticks and canes on the ground. The bird stands over the eggs, shading them with its wings from the blazing hot sun. Out in the open, eggs are more vulnerable to predators, and they have more yolk than usual to help the chicks develop faster.

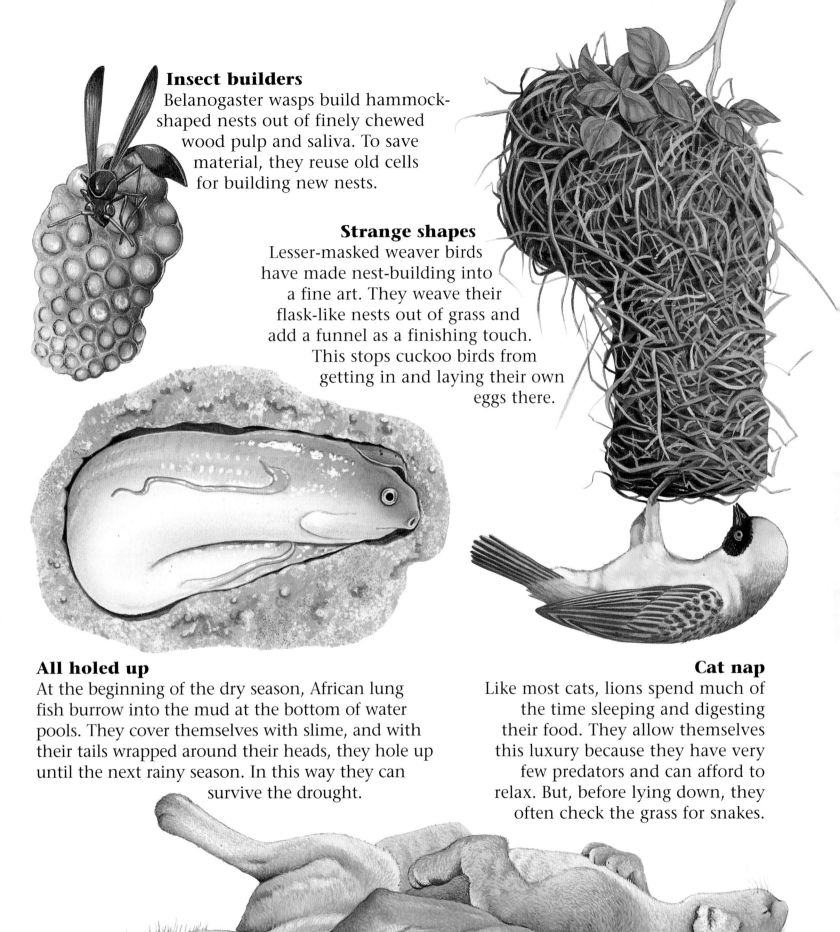

Insect builders
Belanogaster wasps build hammock-shaped nests out of finely chewed wood pulp and saliva. To save material, they reuse old cells for building new nests.

Strange shapes
Lesser-masked weaver birds have made nest-building into a fine art. They weave their flask-like nests out of grass and add a funnel as a finishing touch. This stops cuckoo birds from getting in and laying their own eggs there.

All holed up
At the beginning of the dry season, African lung fish burrow into the mud at the bottom of water pools. They cover themselves with slime, and with their tails wrapped around their heads, they hole up until the next rainy season. In this way they can survive the drought.

Cat nap
Like most cats, lions spend much of the time sleeping and digesting their food. They allow themselves this luxury because they have very few predators and can afford to relax. But, before lying down, they often check the grass for snakes.

Grassland babies

Keeping their young safe on the savanna is a difficult task for animal parents. Many, like frogs and some insects, lay lots of eggs and then leave them. With so many, some are bound to survive. Others give birth to a few babies at a time, and feed and protect them until they are old enough to care for themselves.

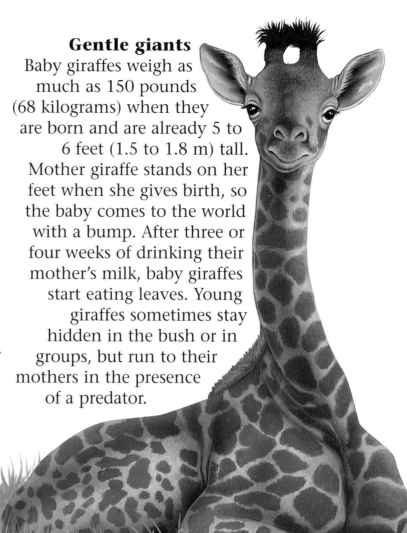

Gentle giants

Baby giraffes weigh as much as 150 pounds (68 kilograms) when they are born and are already 5 to 6 feet (1.5 to 1.8 m) tall. Mother giraffe stands on her feet when she gives birth, so the baby comes to the world with a bump. After three or four weeks of drinking their mother's milk, baby giraffes start eating leaves. Young giraffes sometimes stay hidden in the bush or in groups, but run to their mothers in the presence of a predator.

Fast learner

Zebras live in herds and are very vulnerable to predators. Like all savanna herbivore babies, zebra foals can stand up and run just 20 minutes after they are born!

Free ride

This baby olive baboon is taking a ride on its mother's back. The baby is not strong enough to get around on his own all the time and so relies on his mother to move about.

Play fighting

Lion cubs play with each other and often with their mothers, too. They are not just having fun, but are learning skills they will use later for hunting.

Caring insects
Many insects lay lots of eggs and then abandon them, but not the tsetse fly. A mother tsetse fly looks after just one larvae at a time. The baby larva feeds on a special fluid that comes from the wall of a pouch where it began as an egg.

A long wait
A mother elephant is pregnant for nearly two years before giving birth. Her newborn calf will suckle her milk for about three years and stay close to her for even longer.

Licked clean
Cats spend a lot of time grooming their fur. Mother cheetah is licking her cub, not just to wash him but to strengthen the bond between them. Cheetah cubs have long fluffy manes, making them look bigger than they really are to predators.

A special sort of milk
Newly hatched flamingos have short legs and straight bills and don't look at all like the adults. Their parents regurgitate a special liquid from just above their stomachs and feed it to their babies beak to beak. It is as nutritious as milk.

Scruff of the neck
Like cats, many other mammals carry their young by the scruff of the neck to move them away from danger or to take them to a new home. This doesn't hurt the babies that, like this rat, are very calm.

29

Other grasslands

The African savannas are just one of the world's areas of grasslands. Tropical grasslands also stretch across India, South America, and Australia. The animals and plants found there have had to adapt to the heat and the alternating dry and rainy seasons, just as they have in Africa. Because the living conditions in all of these grasslands are almost identical, several species have evolved in similar ways to survive in the harsh conditions.

The green areas on this map show tropical grasslands across the world.

South America

South American grasslands, called llanos or pampas, are dotted with palm trees, instead of acacias. They are home to some unique animals, like the armadillo, the capybara (sometimes called a water-pig), giant anteaters, and the bush dog. The largest and most dangerous predator is the jaguar, but it now mostly lives in the forests. Large flightless birds called rheas are similar to the ostriches in the African savanna. The South American anteater is similar to the aardvark, with its strong sharp claws, long snout, and long, sticky tongue. Savanna frogs are also a common sight. They have a waxy coating on their skin to help them stay moist.

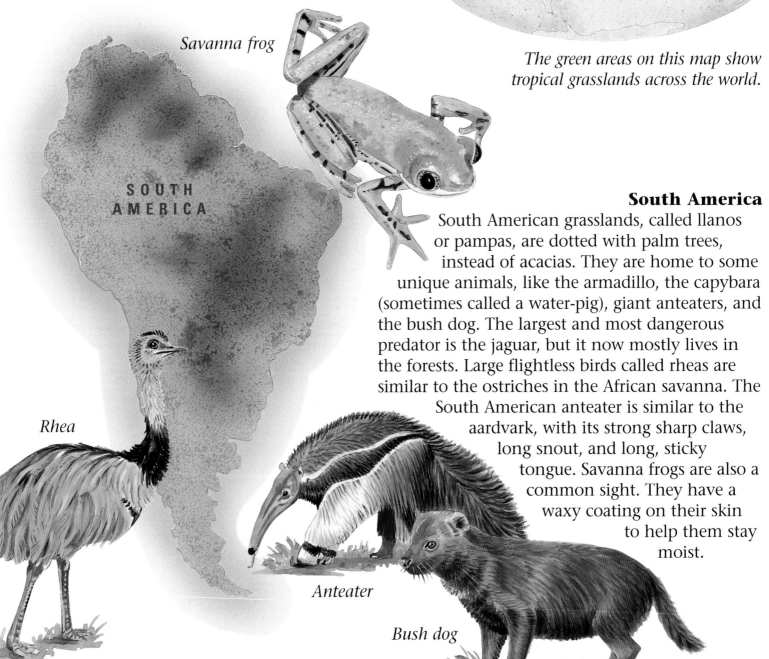

Savanna frog

Rhea

Anteater

Bush dog

India

An amazing sight in the Indian grasslands is the cobra under threat. Raising its body, the cobra opens out its neck like a hood, showing its spectacular markings. The gavial, similar to the crocodile but with a thinner snout, uses its sharp teeth to catch fish and other small animals. The strange, scaly pangolin eats ants, termites and other insects, and it has a long, sticky tongue like the anteater and aardvark. The Indian skies are home to the steppe eagle, that feeds on small animals in the grasslands.

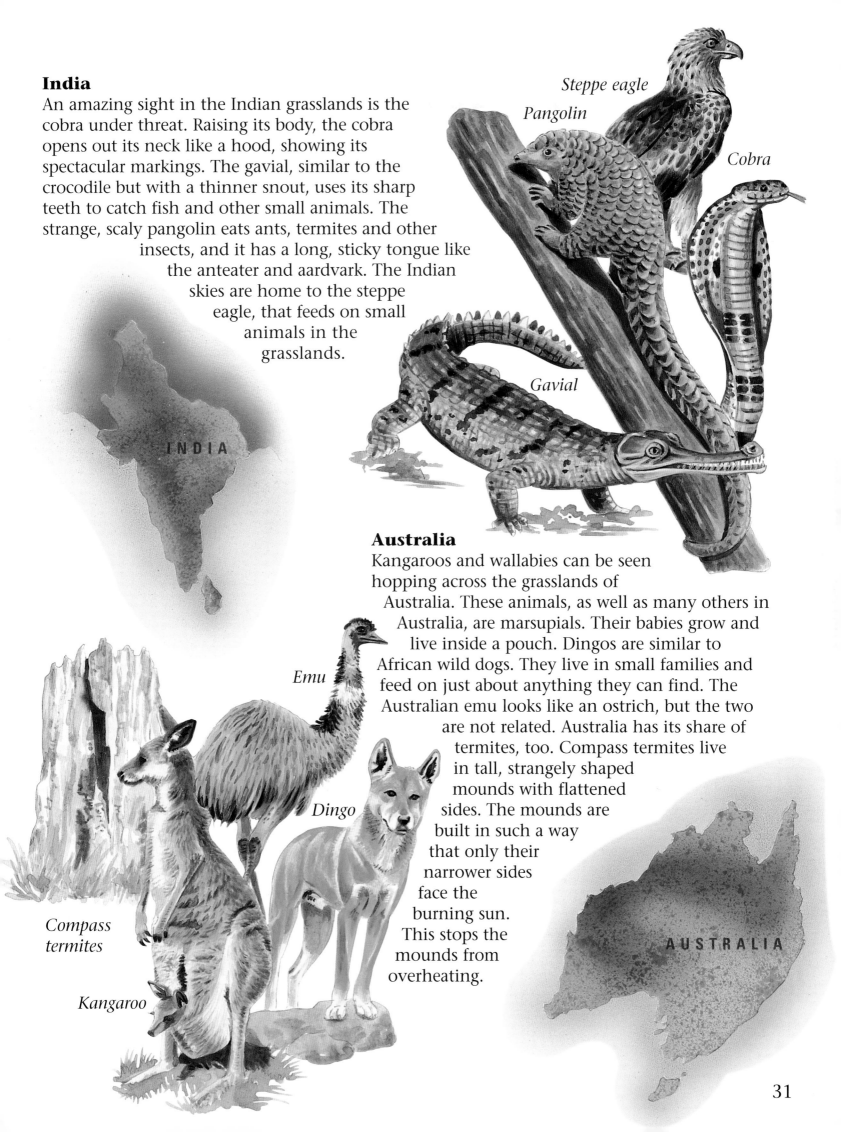

Steppe eagle

Pangolin

Cobra

Gavial

INDIA

Australia

Kangaroos and wallabies can be seen hopping across the grasslands of Australia. These animals, as well as many others in Australia, are marsupials. Their babies grow and live inside a pouch. Dingos are similar to African wild dogs. They live in small families and feed on just about anything they can find. The Australian emu looks like an ostrich, but the two are not related. Australia has its share of termites, too. Compass termites live in tall, strangely shaped mounds with flattened sides. The mounds are built in such a way that only their narrower sides face the burning sun. This stops the mounds from overheating.

Emu

Dingo

Compass termites

Kangaroo

AUSTRALIA

31

In danger

The beautiful grasslands of the savanna have taken millions of years to develop. But their existence is now under threat. The minerals in the ground, the plants that grow there, and the animals that feed on them, all exist in a delicate balance. Unfortunately, humans risk destroying this balance through their farming methods, hunting and poaching, and the destruction of vast areas of land.

Elephant culling

Elephants eat huge amounts of food. They often strip grassland trees and overgraze the plains. Because it would cost governments too much to relocate them, their numbers are controlled by selective hunting.

Poachers

Nowadays more people visit the grasslands with cameras rather than rifles. However, poachers still find a market for elephant tusks, rhino horns, and even hippo teeth. They are sold as ornaments or used to make medicines. Many countries have banned the import of these goods.

Saving the rhinos

Poaching has diminished the rhinoceros population, and they are now facing extinction. Only 2,700 black rhinos and 10,400 white rhinos are left in the world. The International Rhino Foundation is trying to save them by increasing controls on poachers and making people aware of the situation.

Helpful and harmful fires

Natural fires can help make grasslands healthy by stopping too many trees from taking over an area. But the practice of starting fires to clear forests and grasslands for agriculture, called slashing and burning, can cause erosion of the good nutrients in the soil and lead to the formation of deserts.

Animals

Grassland animals are threatened by the ever-growing human population in Africa and its endless need for new farmland. They are also threatened by poachers, despite the existence of natural parks and laws to protect endangered species. Tourism, which brings money to the local people, can also have negative effects because large numbers of motor vehicles on the savannas disturb the animals, especially at critical times such as during mating, birth, and migration.

The effects of farming

The savannas have always been used for agriculture. However, if too much of the land is turned over to growing crops, the grasslands will eventually become deserts. Clearing trees removes the roots that hold the soil together. The wind then blows over the bare expanses, destroying precious fertile layers. When the rains come, they wash all the nutrients and minerals away, leaving the land too poor to farm at all.

Desertification

In the last 50 years, more than 150 million acres (50 million hectares) of grassland south of the Sahara have been turned into desert. Incorrect farming methods are mainly responsible for this (see above right), but stripping the land for firewood is also a factor. When trees are cut down or their branches stripped so that they die, their roots no longer hold the soil firm and it is either blown away by the wind or washed away by the rain.

START

1 What is an herbivore?

2 When do leopards hunt?

3 Are savannas warm all year round?

4 How does the whistling acacia whistle?

5 How do bats find food in the dark?

6 What is a carnivore?

THE AFRICAN GRASSLANDS GAME

21 What is a hardpan?

22 How fast can a cheetah run?

23 What is a rhizome?

24 How does the ostrich escape predators?

25 How does the African honey guide open a bees' nest?

26 Why is the tsetse fly a pest?

27 What is a matriarch?

28 What is a mammal?

29 Why does the African spitting cobra spit?

30 Why do nasute termites have long, hollow snouts?

31 What is a reptile?

9 What does "stotting" mean?

8 Where do gerbils sleep?

How does an elephant drink water?

10 Why do dung beetles collect dung?

11 Why are bald eagles bald?

12 Why do baobab trees have large trunks?

14 How does a giraffe get rid of fleas and ticks?

13 Can an ostrich fly?

16 What do giraffes eat?

15 Why do farmers burn grasslands?

What is a scavenger?

19 Where is the Serengeti National Park?

17

20 Which insects live in the thorns of acacia trees?

18 What does an aardvark eat?

This game can be played by one player, or by two or more players taking turns. You will need a die to roll, and playing pieces (for example, you could use pennies, small stones, or colorful beads.) Each person should choose a playing piece to begin.

Imagine you are a baby crocodile ready to hatch from its egg. The object of the game is to hatch out of your egg and reach the watering hole before any other player. Begin at the small egg buried in the sand marked

START. Throw the die and move forward along the numbered trail of eggs the same number of spaces that the die shows. Answer the question correctly and you may take another turn. If you answer incorrectly, stay where you landed and allow the next person a turn.

Continue in this manner until a player reaches the end of the trail and the last question. In order for you to move forward into the watering hole, you must answer the last question correctly.

32 Do grasslands only have grass in them?

33 How does the African python kill its prey?

34 Can crocodiles chew?

FINISH

Answers to the game

1. An herbivore is an animal that eats only plants.

2. Leopards hunt at night.

3. Yes. Savannas have a warm climate all year round.

4. The whistling acacia tree whistles when the wind blows through its swollen seeds.

5. Bats use echolocation to locate their prey. They send out high-pitched noises through their noses, and the sounds bounce back like echoes.

6. A carnivore is a meat-eating animal.

7. An elephant sucks up water and then squirts it into its mouth through its trunk.

8. Gerbils sleep in burrows which they have made underground.

9. Stotting means springing high into the air.

10. The dung provides protection for the beetle's eggs and is food for the larvae when they hatch.

11. Vultures are bald so that their feathers stay clean when they feed.

12. Baobab trees have large trunks for storing water in the dry season.

13. No. An ostrich cannot fly, but it can run very fast!

14. Oxpeckers sit on the giraffe's back and eat the fleas and ticks.

15. Farmers burn the grasslands to make more space for growing crops.

16. Giraffes eat shoots and leaves from trees.

17. A scavenger is an animal that doesn't kill its own food; it eats the remains of animals that have been left by carnivores.

18. An aadvark eats ants and termites.

19. The Serengeti National Park is in eastern Africa.

20. Ants live in the thorns of acacia trees.

21. Hardpan is the hard top layer of soil in the savanna.

22. A cheetah can run up to 60 miles (about 95 km) per hour.

23. A rhizome is a root that grows out to the side of the grass plant, just below or above the soil.

24. Ostriches hold their heads down so their bodies and long feathers make them appear like bushes on the plain.

25. The African honey guide calls a honey badger to open the nest with its strong claws.

26. The tsetse fly bites humans and animals and spreads a disease called sleeping sickness.

27. A matriarch is the female in charge of finding food and water for the herd.

28. A mammal is an animal that gives birth to live young and rears its offspring on the mother's milk.

29. The African spitting cobra spits venom to blind its prey.

30. Nasute termites squirt an acid spray through their nostrils; the spray gets sticky and traps invading insects such as ants.

31. A reptile is a cold-blooded animal with a hard, scaly skin, like a snake or a crocodile, that lays eggs.

32. No. Grasslands are dotted with bushes and low trees, like the acacia and baobab trees.

33. The African python squeezes its prey to death.

34. No. Crocodiles cannot chew. They swallow their food whole.

Glossary

browse: to feed on leaves, twigs and sparse vegetation.

camouflage: the colors and patterns on something that match or blend in with its surroundings.

carnivores: meat-eating animals, like the tiger.

corpse: a dead body.

cull: to kill surplus animals when their numbers grow too big and the balance of their environment is in danger.

dilating: becoming wider or larger, like the pupil in an eye.

diurnal animals: animals that are active by day and sleep at night, such as the lion.

ecosystem: a place where animals and plants live and interact with their environment and with each other.

echolocation: a type of radar used by bats. They send out high-pitched noises through their noses, and the sounds bounce back like echoes.

extinction: when there are no animals left in a particular species.

equator: an imaginary line that runs around the center of the earth.

herbivores: animals, like the giraffe, that eat only plants.

larva: the name given to an insect after it has hatched out of an egg, but before it has reached its final stage of development. Larvae is the plural of larva.

marsupials: animals, like the kangaroo, whose females have a pouch for carrying their young.

matriarch: the female in charge of finding food and water for the herd.

migration: the movement of animals from one place to another with the seasons. Animals migrate to find food, water, or a climate more suitable to their needs.

nocturnal animals: animals that are active by night and sleep in the day, like the bat.

nutrients: substances which provide food and nourishment.

nutritious food: a type of food that gives plants and animals energy to live and grow.

organisms: the material that makes up a living plant or animal.

poaching: hunting animals using improper methods, like snares and traps. Usually people poach animals to make money from their skins, horns, or other body parts.

predator: animals, like the crocodile, that kill other animals for food.

proboscis: the elongated part of the mouth of animals or insects, like an elephant's trunk.

regurgitate: swallowing food first and then bringing it back up again. Animals often do this to make the food easier for their young to digest.

reptiles: cold-blooded animals with a hard, scaly skin, like a snake or crocodile, that lay eggs.

roost: settle down to sleep, or perch for the night.

saplings: young trees.

savanna: a grassy plain with few or no trees in areas found near the equator.

scavengers: animals, like the jackal, that eat the remains of animals that have been left by carnivores.

lash and burn: the process of clearing vegetation from land by setting fire to it. The land is then turned over for farming.

Index